To my YesKid:

_____

With love from:

_____

Contents

© All rights reserved

Christian Media Publishers,
PO Box 4502, Durbanville, 7551
www.christianmediapublishing.com

Author: Ewald van Rensburg

Illustrations, Design & Layout: Lilani Brits

Publishing Project Manager: Noeline N Neumann

Reg No 2010/008573/07

No part of this publication may be reproduced
by any means – electronically or otherwise –
without the prior written permission of the publisher.

Text: Maranatha Publishing: Used by kind agreement.

Printed in Malaysia through PrettyInPress Productions.

First Editon, second printing, 2013
ISBN 978-1-920460-53-2

CMP-kids books have been developed with your child's
(·ıİİ) **developmental phases** and (✛) **unique temperament** in mind.
For a full explanation of the **unique temperament** and **developmental
phases** icons visit the CMP website **www.cmpublishing.co.za**

YesKids
Bible Stories
- about Obedience -

Kids saying YES! Doing the Right Thing

Written by Ewald van Rensburg
Illustrations by Lilani Brits

cmp
christian media publishing Kids

pointing children in the **right direction**

1. Always listen to God!

(Genesis 3)

God put Adam and Eve in a beautiful place called the Garden of Eden.
It was a lovely place to live. God said to them, "You can eat everything you find here. But there is one special tree; you may not eat the fruit growing on this tree. If you do you will surely die."

One day the evil devil disguised himself as a snake. He talked to Eve and told her terrible lies. He said, "You can eat the fruit on this special tree. You will not die, like God says you will."

Then Adam and Eve ate some fruit from the tree. God was very sad when he saw that they had disobeyed him. As a result, they had to leave the Garden of Eden.

Bad things happen when we don't listen to God. Luckily for us, Jesus made everything right again when he gave his life for us.

Come, let's pray together:

Dear Father, please help me
to always listen to you.
Amen.

Jesus washed away our sins.
Always listen to God.

7

2. God makes a donkey talk!

(Numbers 22)

King Balak offered to pay Balaam a lot of money to say bad things about God's chosen people. But God decided to stop Balaam.

Balaam was riding his donkey on his way to King Balak. Suddenly an angel of the Lord appeared in the road. He was holding a sword.

Only the donkey could see the angel.
Balaam could not see him at all.

Three times, the donkey turned off
the road to avoid the angel.
Each time Balaam hit the donkey.

Then the Lord opened Balaam's eyes, and suddenly he also saw the angel. The angel said to him, "From now on you will say what God tells you to say." And that is exactly what Balaam did.

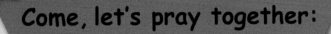

Come, let's pray together:

Dear God, help me not to say nasty things about other people. Amen.

Jesus does not like it when we say nasty things about other people.

3. With God's help
(Esther 1 - 10)

Esther was a very beautiful woman. She was so beautiful that the king of Persia made her his wife and queen.

One day her uncle Mordecai, came to visit her. He said to her, "All the Jewish people — including you and me — are in serious trouble. That wicked man Haman, wants to kill all of us. He told the king lies about us and now the king has made a law saying that on a particular day all the Jews must be murdered."

Mordecai fell to his knees in front of Esther and said, "Please Esther, help us. Only you can save us."

Esther invited the king and the evil Haman to dinner.

She told the king about Haman's plans to kill her and her people.

The king was very angry with Haman. He made a new law that saved the Jews. The Jews were so happy they all danced in the streets.

Esther was a brave woman who saved her people with God's help.

Come, let's pray together:

Dear God, I help other people because I love you so much.
Amen.

God uses ordinary people, like you and me and Esther, to help others.

15

4. The ten girls

(Matthew 25)

Jesus told this story too ...

Ten girls with oil lamps were waiting for a special visitor to arrive.
They did not know when the visitor would be there. They kept their lamps burning the whole time, because it was dark.

Sadly, only five of the girls had been clever enough to bring extra oil with them. Before long, all ten girls began to yawn and fall asleep.

Suddenly someone shouted, "Here he is, the important visitor is here!" Quickly the five clever girls filled their lamps with extra oil and lit them.

The other five girls had to run to the nearest shop to buy more oil.

The important visitor was very happy to see the five clever girls and they had a lovely party. There were delicious things to eat and to drink.

When the other five girls arrived, it was too late to join the party. They missed all the fun.

Come, let's pray together:

Jesus, I want to bring you joy and have a joyful time with you in heaven one day. Amen.

Always do your best for Jesus, because he always does his best for you.

19

5. Bad Zacchaeus becomes Good Zacchaeus (Luke 19)

Zacchaeus was a very rich man who lived in Jericho. Nobody liked him because he was nasty to other people. Zacchaeus. He wanted to see Jesus very badly, but he was too short to see over the heads of the people in the crowd.

The people pushed him out of the way because nobody wanted to stand near the nasty Zacchaeus. So Zacchaeus climbed into a nearby tree. From there he could see Jesus clearly. Jesus saw him straight away.

The people were all astonished when Jesus began to talk to Zacchaeus. And Zacchaeus was amazed when Jesus came to his house to eat a meal with him. From that day onwards "Bad Zacchaeus" became "Good Zacchaeus", and he was always ready to help everyone.

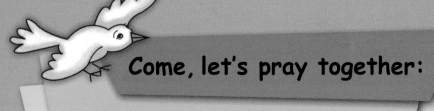

Come, let's pray together:

Lord Jesus, I want to help
other people too.
Amen.

People who love Jesus enjoy helping other people.

Guidelines for parents

Faith Icon
The formation of faith is indeed unique to each child; there are however general characteristics which apply to all children. There are three main ways that children develop faith:

- Parents regularly reading the Bible, telling Bible and other faith based stories, praying together and doing faith building activities with their children (such as the ones found in this book).
- Children ask questions – parents need to take these questions seriously and answer them according to the child's level of understanding.
- Children follow the example of those caring for them.

Emotional intelligence icon
We experience emotions long before we learn the language to be able to express how we are feeling. Therefore it is important that children are taught to verbalise what they are feeling. Use the illustrations accompanying the stories and ask your child how they think the people or animals in the picture feel. This helps them become aware of their own emotions as well as those of others. It provides a learning opportunity where the child can learn appropriate words to express how they are feeling.

Reading icon
A wonderful world opens up for your child when they start learning to read. Enjoy every moment of this exciting adventure with your child. Let them sit on your lap where they can be comfortable and feel safe and secure. Open the book holding it so that you can both see the pages. Read clearly and with enthusiasm. As you know you can read the same story over and over. Point out where you are reading with your finger as you go along. This will help your child to begin to see the relationship between letters, sounds, words and their meaning. Encourage your child's attempts at reading – even of it sounds like gibberish.

Listening skills icon
Listening is an important learning and development skill. You can help develop this skill in your child by encouraging them to listen attentively, and understand what they are hearing. Let them look at the illustrations and then use their imagination to tell the story back to you in their own words. You can also encourage them to do this by asking questions relating to the story. Yet another way is to leave out words from a story the child knows well and let them fill in the missing words.

Vocabulary icon
Use every opportunity to build your child's vocabulary – it is a lifelong gift which you are giving to them. Start with everyday objects and people in the illustrations in books. Point at the picture, say the word, form a short sentence using the word. Repeat it again and then let your child say the word. Try to use the word in another context – if there is a tent in the picture you are looking at then say: we sleep in a tent when we go camping.

Numeracy skills icon
It is important for your child develop numeracy skills. Play simple games such as: "How many ducks are there in the picture? If we add two more ducks how many are there now? Then if three fly away? (use your fingers to illustrate this) How many are left? They also need to recognise the shape of numbers – cut large numbers from cardboard – let your child play with these – place the numbers in order forming a line from one to ten.